If a Stoic was a Poet

Em Hli

BookLeaf Publishing

India | USA | UK

Presentation by *BookLeaf Publishing*

Web: www.bookleafpub.com

E-mail: info@bookleafpub.com

ISBN: 9789363309982

First edition 2024

ACKNOWLEDGEMENT

This book is dedicated to all the stoics in my life long before I knew the word, stoic. The experiences of stoicism from these stoics are what kept me grounded and going.

We are like the Season

Life is always at stake but for life' sake we live
life one day at a time
So at times, we mistake the subtleness of life as
insignificance instead of great importance
But we must caution life is all rehearsals not
grand moments
And we are only here for a season

Success

The fruition of today started years ago,
therefore freedom is not free,
Freedom is consistency, discipline,
deliberateness and preparation.
So when people talk about success like it is
overnight
know that success is overtime.

Problems

Don't personalize problems, solve them
But some are not for solving or dissolving
Some are there so that we can be clear about
who we are and what we are
Because problems are not always obstacles
Some are challenges that we must overcome in
order to become
So why make things personal
Let's never dread about things or people, if we
can't be part of the solutions

What We Forgot

Some plan for the future
While I live for the moment
But what we forgotten, being present

Some walk around winter like it's summer
While I stop and take a breath
But what we forgotten, genuine character

Some study and gain skills
While I wait and observe
For what we forgotten, self-education

Some say you live and you learn
While I say, we stay sane or same
For what we forgotten, life is whole and we are
just a small fraction

Be Fully Present

5

Confidence comes from over preparation
Consistency plus discipline equals freedom
Deliberate practice beats talents
Greatness comes out of goodness
And happiness comes from presence
However, success doesn't always come from
genius but genuineness
So, be the most present and live life moment by
moment

Life

Life is great if you believe in greatness.

Life is beautiful if you choose to see the beauty.

Life is wonderful if you never lose your sense of wonder.

But more than anything, Life will always be yours for the taking.

So will you make something out of Life

Or is Life something that happened to you?

Start Today

There is nothing special about every day
But today when your efforts exceed your fear
when you believe in the process
when you develop a routine
when you condition yourself
when you do the work
That is when your life will begin
So start now,
Because today is just like any other day

Genuine Presence

Today your presence surrenders to the mercy of
character
And you don't hide your doubt and fear with a
bitter smile
You break down and cry
You know how to show vulnerability
You model mental toughness which is the most
ruthless strength
Your heart is always full and your head is clear
and free
You are not bothered by yesterday or tomorrow
You work endlessly on what is in front of you
until completion
Then you give your best to the next
And you carry light and lightly for you know
time is among us all
So if nothing beats time, it is your genuine
presence

Heart Burning Desire

Good thing that you have a burning desire,
But if you don't put that burning desire into your head,
And eventually to your hands
Then it might just burn you to keep it burning in your heart.

Your Life

Your life is important, not only when you start
doing important things
Your life is precious, not only when your life is
at its last stage
Life is short only in moments when time seems
to be relative
But note, life is forever and it all starts with you,
so when you get better so does your life

The Fear of Time

One day Change told me,
"Stay consistent."
But Time left me a notice,
"Today will never come again, but tomorrow is
my promise to you."
So I learnt how to put things off.
Soon my days turned into years.
Change cautioned,
"Your time is limited, live in the moment."
But Time told me,
"You have a whole life ahead of you."
I took a deep breath and relaxed.
Change panicked,
"Do not take time for granted, go get started."
 I reassured Change,
"I have all the time in the world."
Time laughed,
"That's right!"
Change was disheartened,
"If you don't make space for change now,
someday you will have to make time and you
might not have the time."
That someday came and Time whispered,
"Your time is up."
I woke up,

"What time is it?"
My mom bent over,
"Why? Where are you going? It's a Saturday."
I felt a sense of relief. I looked at the time, 6:38
AM. I looked in the mirror, I am only 10.
But I was sure in my dream I was in my 20s, 30s
or maybe even 50s.
So I looked at my mom dead in the eye,
"I am scared of time."
My mom laughed,
"Don't be honey, time comes one day at a time."

Be Nothing but Good

On good days, let them be good

On bad days, let there still be good

Time will defer everything so don't let your life
stalls

Let there be good things to talk about and do

For life is too short but we don't have to fall
short

Let's be good or be nothing at all

Our Presence

We are part of the past, present and future
Yet life is situational
And we are emotional
So at times we forget the fragility of time
But if we are lucky we get to see life past a
certain point
For life is like an emotional journey that always
stay in motion with a timestamp
But we can't take life personally
Or even make life personal
But to find meaning,
We live our everyday with purpose and urgency
With lots of mercy, compassion and empathy
And be present with our unique character and
genuine nature
So even if we don't become legends at least we
left a tradition
And if we don't live forever
At least people can bear with our absence
knowing that our once presence was nothing
more but subtle boldness, wit, warmth, kindness
and humor

When We Don't Make It

When we exceed in excellence
Let that be our energy that we put out and not
our ego

When we make a difference in others lives
Let that be the success of happiness

When we give people something good to talk
about
Let that be a reminder that hard work pays off

But when we don't make it
Let's not beat ourselves up
Let's just start over again
And give ourselves the same goodness that we
would give others
if they were to do the same

Our Indifference

I don't expect anyone to be like me
I let others present themselves
Just like I don't hold them to the same standard
But I still hold them in the best regards
Because I know that our differences are not what
make us different,
it is our indifference

Freedom

Everyone works to achieve financial freedom
thinking that they will be free
But freedom is not dependent on anything or
anyone
Freedom is you enjoying what you do,
you, being authentic,
you, being present,
and you, being healthy and happy

Move On

Whenever you go off tangent
We all know you don't have bad intentions
But your high regards, will it get you very far?
Even if you really care,
Where is your compassion for yourself?
How many times do you have to be miserable
because of them?
How many times do you have to pick yourself
up piece by piece because they let you down?
How many times do you have to put up a fight
every time for the right reason with the wrong
person?
And how many more times do you have to
remind yourself, This is it, I am done?
Too many to count
So?
Whenever you want to go off tangent
Note that your high regards can just be simply a
yours truly and leave it at that remark
For it is tough, but even tougher when you really
don't know who you are versus when people
don't give you the same regards or know what
you are truly made of
Carry on

Work Hard on You

Work hard on yourself, not others
Because when something goes down
You'll find yourself complaining first, not others
So learn to mind your shoulders
Because it is not the weight but the mass you
have to worry about
So be prepared to be calm
Because only then will you be able to withstand
the commotion,
and not be drowned the opinions

Self-Control

When we lose control
Remember it was never ours to begin with
Except the discomfort we avoided
The old habits we still engaged in
The slow inconsistent progress of our long
overdue project
The non-supportive circle of friends we still
surrounded ourselves with
The lack of clarity in our goal setting
And the temporary motivation that we hold
ourselves to
So when nothing else seems to be in our control
Let's remember we still have our self-control

To Start is to not Be Delayed

There is no time deposit slip
And our process is still pending instead of in
progress
And we can't help but wonder if it was our
apathy or empathy that caused us to delay?
Are we scared of the final product or the
process?
Or do we have a lack of clarity, urgency or not
enough purpose?
But before we know it,
We don't have time for anything
Yet we always manage to say, "I will get to it
later"
And we know our life is always moving forward
Yet we use "someday" like it will come
But the truth is,
It was never the execution part,
It was the getting started that always get delayed

Fear

We all have lived through times when
We were confident and brave,
Anxious and vulnerable,
Scared and furious.
But we live in a world where fear is not an
immediate threat but chronic deadlines.
So, we should fear not the adversity, but our own
will and mind.